1 MONTH OF
FREE
READING

at
www.ForgottenBooks.com

By purchasing this book you are eligible for one month membership to ForgottenBooks.com, giving you unlimited access to our entire collection of over 1,000,000 titles via our web site and mobile apps.

To claim your free month visit:
www.forgottenbooks.com/free1125465

ISBN 978-0-331-44827-6
PIBN 11125465

This book is a reproduction of an important historical work. Forgotten Books uses
state-of-the-art technology to digitally reconstruct the work, preserving the original format
whilst repairing imperfections present in the aged copy. In rare cases, an imperfection in
the original, such as a blemish or missing page, may be replicated in our edition. We do,
however, repair the vast majority of imperfections successfully; any imperfections that
remain are intentionally left to preserve the state of such historical works.

Historic, archived document

Do not assume content reflects current
scientific knowledge, policies, or practices.

THE *Fats and Oils* SITUATION

BUREAU OF AGRICULTURAL ECONOMICS
UNITED STATES DEPARTMENT OF AGRICULTURE

FOS-66   BAE   AUGUST 1942

IN THIS ISSUE:
PRODUCTION AND UTILIZATION OF PEANUTS
AND PEANUT OIL

PEANUTS PICKED AND THRESHED, AND PEANUT CRUSHINGS, UNITED STATES, 1919-42

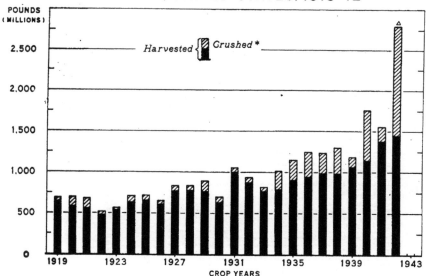

Harvested / Crushed*

POUNDS (MILLIONS)

*YEAR BEGINNING OCTOBER   △ PRODUCTION, AUGUST 1 INDICATION, CRUSHINGS, ESTIMATED

U. S. DEPARTMENT OF AGRICULTURE   NEG. 42528   BUREAU OF AGRICULTURAL ECONOMICS

FROM 1919 TO 1941 PRODUCTION OF PICKED AND THRESHED PEANUTS MORE THAN DOUBLED. IN 1942 IT WILL PROBABLY ALMOST DOUBLE AGAIN, REACHING 2.8 BILLION POUNDS. A TOTAL OF 1,350 MILLION POUNDS OF PEANUTS (FARMERS' STOCK BASIS) MAY BE CRUSHED, WITH A PRODUCTION OF ABOUT 400 MILLION POUNDS OF PEANUT OIL.

Table 1.- Wholesale price per pound of fats and oils at specified markets, and index
numbers of prices, July 1940 and 1941, May-July 1942

PRICES

Item	July 1940	July 1941	1942 May	1942 June	1942 July
	Cents	Cents	Cents	Cents	Cents
Butter, 92-score, Chicago ....:	26.5	34.3	37.3	36.2	37.6
Butter, 92-score, New York ....:	27.0	34.8	37.8	36.8	38.2
Oleomargarine, dom. veg., Chicago ....:	15.0	15.7	19.0	19.0	19.0
Compounds (animal and veg. cooking fats), Chicago ....:	9.2	14.8	17.0	17.0	17.0
Lard, loose, Chicago ....:	4.9	9.5	11.4	11.8	11.9
Lard, prime steam, tierces, Chicago ....:	5.8	10.2	12.6	12.6	12.8
Lard, refined, cartons, Chicago ....:	6.2	10.9	14.6	14.5	14.5
Oleo oil, extra, tierces, Chicago ....:	7.0	10.4	13.0	13.0	13.0
Oleostearine, bbl., N.Y. ....:	5.5	9.8	10.5	10.5	10.5
Tallow, edible, Chicago ....:	4.2	8.1	---	---	9.9
Corn oil, crude, tanks, f.o.b. mills ....:	5.4	11.9	12.8	12.7	12.7
Corn oil, refined, bbl., N.Y. ....:	8.4	15.1	15.0	15.0	15.5
Cottonseed oil, crude, tanks, f.o.b. S. E. mills ....:	5.4	10.6	12.7	12.8	12.8
Cottonseed oil, p.s.y., tank cars, N.Y. ....:	6.0	11.8	14.1	13.8	14.0
Peanut oil, crude, tanks, f.o.b. mills ....:	5.8	11.1	13.0	13.0	12.9
Peanut oil, dom. refined, bbl., N.Y. ....:	8.9	---	17.0	17.0	17.0
Soybean oil, crude, tank cars, midwestern mills ....:	4.6	9.8	11.8	11.6	11.2
Soybean oil, dom., crude, drums, N.Y. ....:	6.2	12.3	13.0	13.0	12.8
Soybean oil, refined, drums, N.Y. ....:	7.1	12.7	14.2	14.2	14.2
Babassu oil, tanks, f.o.b. mills, Pacific Coast ....:	---	9.1	10.7	---	---
Olive oil, edible, drums, N.Y. ....:	30.7	72.7	72.7	66.3	61.6
Olive oil, inedible, drums, N.Y. ....:	19.2	52.3	58.3	56.7	56.7
Olive-oil foots, prime, drums, N.Y. ....:	9.0	17.0	19.5	19.5	19.5
Palm oil, Niger, crude, drums, N.Y. 1/ ....:	7.4	9.9	12.0	12.0	12.1
Rape oil, drums, N.Y. ....:	15.0	15.2	15.5	15.5	15.8
Rape oil, blown, drums, N.Y. ....:	17.5	17.5	18.2	18.2	18.2
Teaseed oil, crude, drums, N.Y. ....:	12.5	22.7	---	---	30.0
Tallow, inedible, Chicago ....:	3.8	7.6	9.3	---	8.4
Grease, A white, Chicago ....:	3.8	7.8	9.6	9.6	9.0
Menhaden oil, crude, tanks, f.o.b. Baltimore ....:	4.7	7.8	8.9	8.9	8.9
Sardine oil, crude, tanks, Pacific Coast ....:	5.0	8.0	8.9	8.9	8.9
Whale oil, refined, bleached winter, drums, N.Y. ....:	9.5	10.5	11.1	11.1	11.1
Linseed oil, raw, tank cars, Minneapolis ....:	8.7	10.4	13.1	12.8	12.6
Linseed oil, raw, drums, carlots, N.Y. ....:	9.3	11.4	14.2	14.0	13.8
Perilla oil, drums, N.Y. ....:	18.8	20.0	24.6	24.6	24.6
Oiticica oil, drums, N.Y. ....:	18.0	20.6	25.2	25.2	25.1
Tung oil, drums, N.Y. ....:	25.6	32.2	40.2	40.2	39.6
Castor oil, No. 3, bbl., N.Y. ....:	12.2	11.5	13.8	13.8	13.8
Castor oil, dehydrated, drums, carlots, N.Y. ....:	15.7	15.7	18.6	18.6	18.6
Cod-liver oil, med. U.S.P. bbl., N.Y. ....:	29.3	35.8	36.4	36.4	36.4
Cod oil, Newfoundland, drums, N.Y. ....:		10.5	11.5	12.0	12.0

INDEX NUMBERS (1924-29 = 100)

Eight domestic fats and oils (1910-14 = 100) ....:	79	116	133	130	133
Eight domestic fats and oils ....:	56	82	94	92	94
All fats and oils (27 items) ....:	61	90	102	100	101
Grouped by origin:					
Animal fats ....:	57	79	89	87	89
Marine animal oils ....:	88	115	126	127	127
Vegetable oils, domestic ....:	62	109	130	128	129
Vegetable oils, foreign ....:	88	139	160	156	148
Grouped by use:					
Butter ....:	60	78	85	83	86
Butter, seasonally adjusted ....:		84	93	90	
Lard ....:		78	96	96	
Food fats, other ....:	66	124	112	138	138
Soap fats ....:	59	108	128	128	120
Drying oils ....:	91	112	140	138	136
Miscellaneous oils ....:	98	102	114	116	116

Prices compiled from Oil, Paint and Drug Reporter, The National Provisioner, and reports of the Agricultural Marketing
Administration and Bureau of Labor Statistics. Prices quoted include excise taxes and duties where applicable. Index
numbers for earlier years beginning 1910 are given in Technical Bulletin No. 737 (1940) and The Fats and Oils Situation
beginning December 1940.

1/ Three-cent processing tax added to price as originally quoted.

Summary

Production of the principal domestic oilseeds in 1942 now seems likely to exceed earlier expectations. August 1 indications point to increases over last year of 22 percent in the cottonseed crop, of 33 percent in flaxseed, of 74 percent in soybeans, and of 90 percent in peanuts. Production of animal fats and oils also is increasing. Total production of fats and oils from domestic materials in 1942-43 may total 11.9 billion pounds, more than 2 billion pounds in excess of the output of the 1941-42 crop year, and more than 50 percent above the 1936-40 average.

Despite the record-breaking oil crops expected, the prospective "tight" fats and oils supply situation has not been completely relieved. Imports of fats and oils from the Far East have been greatly reduced in recent months and scarcity of shipping space may restrict imports from other areas. Exports of fats and oils under lend-lease, moreover, will be materially larger in 1942-43 than a year earlier. And with rising consumer purchasing power and maximum retail prices in effect, domestic consumption of fats and oils is expected to increase in the next several months unless restricted by Government action.

Price changes in July were mixed. The Government support price for 92-score butter at Chicago was raised 3 cents on July 22 to 39 cents per pound. A few days earlier quotations for inedible tallow and greases had declined about 1 cent per pound on the announcement of lowered price ceilings for these fats effective August 1. Prices of lard and refined edible oils strengthened slightly in July, reflecting large Government purchases and reduced factory supplies.

— August 20, 1942

REVIEW OF RECENT DEVELOPMENTS

BACKGROUND.- Prices of fats and oils, which were unusually low in 1939 and 1940, advanced sharply in the first
half of 1941, reflecting a tight shipping situation for
imported materials, marked improvement in domestic demand,
and Government purchases of lard for export. In the first
quarter of 1942 further advances were made, notably by
lard and linseed oil. Maximum wholesale prices for fats
and oils were first established on December 13, 1941. On
January 2, 1942, the maximum price schedule was revised
upward. On February 4, a further increase in the maximum
price of lard was made, and the ceiling on linseed oil was
removed. Effective May 18, ceiling prices were established
on retail prices of fats and oils, except butter and linseed oil, at highest prices charged during March 1942.

Price Changes Mixed in July

The index of wholesale prices of 27 major fats and oils advanced 1
point in July to 101 percent of the 1924-29 level, compared with 90 percent
in July 1941. Price changes during the month were mixed. Inedible tallow
and grease prices declined about 1 cent per pound on the announcement of
lowered ceilings effective August 1, but butter averaged about 1.4 cents per
pound higher than a month earlier. After moving gradually upward during the
first half of the month, the price of 92-score butter at Chicago advanced 1.5
cents per pound on July 22 to the new support level of 39 cents and in early
August reached 40.5 cents.

Large Government purchases of edible fats and oils, together with de-
clining stocks of lard, led to a slight advance in prices of lard and of
refined edible oils in July. At the end of the month lard prices were at
ceiling levels. The price of crude soybean oil at mills averaged lower in
July than in June but strengthened toward the end of the month and continued
strong in early August. Small changes, apparently reflecting changes in the
basis of quotation, occurred in some of the quoted prices of imported fats
and oils and of marine animal oils when specific maximum prices for these fats
and oils were announced by the Office of Price Administration. The price of
rapeseed oil advanced 0.5 cents per pound late in July under the higher maximum price which was set to allow for an increase in procurement costs since
the old ceiling was established.

Support Price for Butter Raised

On July 21 the Department of Agriculture announced a new support price
of 39 cents per pound for 92-score butter at Chicago, 3 cents above the former
support price in effect since late March, but only 1-1/2 cents above the market
price prevailing when the announcement was made. New support prices also were
announced for other manufactured dairy products. Prices for evaporated milk
and roller-process dry skim milk were reduced, while prices for cheese and
spray-process dry skim milk were increased. The purpose of the new support
prices is to encourage the dairy industry to maintain the present high rate

of production of dairy products but at the same time to bring about a shift
in the utilization of milk in line with present domestic and lend-lease
requirements. More butter and dry skim milk are needed but less evaporated
milk. Cheese requirements remain unchanged. Production of butter (including
farm butter) is expected to total about 2,250 million pounds in 1942, slightly less than in 1941, although output in the second half of the year may be
about 5 percent larger than a year earlier. Butter production is expected to
be materially increased in 1943.

Ceiling Prices for Inedible
Tallow and Greases Reduced

New maximum prices for inedible tallow and greases averaging 1 cent per
pound lower than the previous ceilings were announced July 20 by the Office of
Price Administration in Amendment No. 6 to Revised Price Schedule 53. Although
August 1 was set as the effective date of the amendment with respect to inedible tallow and greases, market quotations immediately declined to the new
ceiling levels. Purpose of the "roll-back" was to reestablish a normal manu-
facturing margin for soap. Earlier this year, in a move to allow distributors
a normal margin under the maximum retail prices for soap established at highest
March levels, manufacturers representing more than 80 percent of the soap
business rescinded price increases made on February 28 in line with increasing
raw material costs. As a result, manufacturers' selling prices have been low
in relation to prices of fats and oils used in soap.

In 1941 inedible tallow and greases accounted for 56 percent of the
total fats, oils, and rosin used in the manufacture of soap. In 1942 and 1943,
with supplies of coconut and other important soap oils greatly reduced because
of loss of imports, inedible tallow and greases will constitute a still greater
portion. Inedible tallow and greases are minor byproducts of livestock
slaughter, and the reduction in prices is not expected to have an appreciable
effect on prices received by farmers for meat animals. The maximum price for
edible tallow remains virtually unchanged with the ceiling at Chicago placed
at 9-7/8 cents per pound. The revised maximum price for No. 1 tallow (inedible
at Chicago is placed at 8-3/8 cents, and for grease, A white, Chicago, the revised price is 8-3/4 cents per pound.

Specific Maximum Prices Set for Certain
Imported Oils and Marine Animal Oils

In addition to establishing new maximum prices for tallow and greases,
Amendment No. 6 to Revised Price Schedule 53 established specific maximum
prices on 19 imported vegetable oils and 7 marine animal oils, effective
July 25. Except for rapeseed oil, the new ceilings are at the same level as
the old. Unlike the former ceilings, they are not based on individual seller's
prices during a certain period but are stated in cents per pound for specified
grades at specified locations and in specified containers. The maximum prices
established in the amendment are as follows:

```
Crude, Manila ...........................................  8.35
Crude, Manila, San Francisco .........................  8.00
Cochin type ...............................................  9.35
Cochin type, San Francisco ...........................  9.00
Refined Edible, f.o.b., New York, ex tax ...........  9.85
Refined Edible, f.o.b., San Francisco, ex tax ......  9.50
Palm oil – African:
   Soft, basis 12% f.f.a. ...............................  8.25
   Semi, basis 35% f.f.a. ...............................  8.25
   Niger, or hard, basis over 45% f.f.a. .............  8.25
   Congo Plantation, basis 10% f.f.a. ...............  8.32
   Malayan and Sumatra, basis 5% f.f.a. ...........  8.50
Palm kernel oil, crude ..................................  8.35
Rapeseed oil, denatured ................................ 11.50
Teaseed oil, crude, in drums ......................... 30.00
```

<u>Imported vegetable oils, tank cars, f.o.b.</u>
<u>New York, duties and taxes paid, cents per pound</u>

```
Andiroba, drums, carlots ............................... 11.00
Babassu oil ................................................ 11.10
Castor oil:
   No. 1 ................................................... 13.05
   No. 3 ................................................... 12.75
   Dehydrated, bodied ................................. 17.85
Cohune oil ................................................ 11.10
Muru-muru oil ........................................... 14.03
Oiticica oil:
   Commercial grade, liquid .......................... 25.00
   Condensed, drums, carlots ....................... 23.00
Ouricuri oil .............................................. 11.10
Pataua oil ................................................ 40.00
Perilla oil, crude ........................................ 24.50
Sesame oil ............................................... 14.30
Sunflower seed oil, semi-refined ................... 14.30
Tucum oil ................................................ 12.68
Tung oil (Chinawood oil), drums, carlots .......... 39.00
Ucuhuba crude vegetable tallow, barrels or drums,
   carlots ..................................................  8.75
```

<u>Marine animal oils, tank cars, f.o.b. American ports,</u>
<u>duties and taxes paid, cents per pound</u>

```
Whale oil, crude, No. 1 ................................ 11.25
Sperm oil, crude, No. 1 ...............................  7.75
Seal oil, No. 1 ..........................................  8.90
Menhaden, crude, f.o.b. producer's plant,
   Atlantic coast .........................................  8.90
Sardine oil, crude, f.o.b. producer's plant,
   Pacific coast ..........................................  8.90
Sardine oil, hydrogenated 52°, f.o.b. producer's
   plant, Pacific coast ................................. 10.90
Herring oil, crude, f.o.b. Seattle ...................  8.90
```

Normal differentials for grade, location, and type of container may be applied to these prices. Duties, processing and import taxes may be added to the above prices where applicable.

Production of Fats and Oils up Slightly in First Half-Year

Factory production of fats and oils, including creamery butter, in the first 6 months of 1942 reached nearly 4.8 billion pounds, about 5 percent above the total for the first 6 months of 1941. 1/ Estimated production from domestic materials at 4.5 billion pounds was about 8 percent greater, but estimated production from imported materials at 295 million pounds was 28 percent less.

Decreases of 137 and 88 million pounds occurred in the production of cottonseed and peanut oils, respectively, as a result of smaller cottonseed and peanut crops in 1941 than in 1940. With reduced supplies of copra, production of coconut oil was 104 million pounds less in the first half of 1942 than a year earlier. These decreases were more than offset by an increase of 136 million pounds in the factory production of lard (including rendered pork fat), approximately 240 million pounds in the production of inedible tallow and greases, 120 million pounds in the production of linseed oil, and increases in the production of soybean oil, corn oil, and castor oil. Increased livestock slaughter in the first half of 1942 and a record soybean crop in 1941 account for the increases in production of lard, tallow, greases, and soybean oil, but demand factors were mainly responsible for the other increases. The heavy demand for drying oils and the shortage of tung, perilla, and oiticica oils induced large imports of flaxseed and castor beans. A strong demand for corn products, including corn starch and corn sugar, was chiefly responsible for an increased output of corn oil, a byproduct of the corn-grinding industry.

June 30 Stocks of Fats and Oils Reduced

Despite a high rate of production of primary fats and oils in the second half of 1941 and in the first half of 1942, factory and warehouse stocks of fats and oils on June 30 totaled slightly more than 2.0 billion pounds (crude basis) -- 9 percent less this year than last, and smaller than in any year since 1937. Reflecting heavy production, stocks of soybean oil, linseed oil, and corn oil, were 82, 75, and 25 million pounds, respectively, greater than last year. Stocks of babassu oil and rapeseed oil were also substantially higher. On the other hand, cottonseed oil stocks at 449 million pounds were slightly lower than a year earlier, and stocks of oils imported mainly from the Far East were materially smaller. The combined stocks of coconut oil and palm oil on July 1 amounted to 246 million pounds (crude basis), about 21 percent less than last year. Stocks of tung oil, at 32 million pounds, have not declined greatly, as the use of this oil is restricted to military purposes, but stocks of perilla oil at 3 million pounds are near the vanishing point.

1/ Totals include estimates for unreported production of inedible tallow and greases in small rendering plants and on farms, but are incomplete with respect to lard and butter.

Substantial declines have also occurred in stocks of lard, inedible tallow and greases, and peanut oil. Smaller stocks of peanut oil reflect reduced production in 1941, but the reduction in lard and tallow stocks has occurred in the face of increased production. Cold storage stocks of lard (including rendered pork fat) were reported at 102 million pounds, compared with 383 million pounds a year earlier. August 1 figures show a further decline to 99 million pounds, with nearly 22 million pounds out of this total held by the Federal Surplus Commodity Corporation, primarily in connection with lend-lease operations. Factory and warehouse stocks of inedible tallow and greases at 334 million pounds were 16 percent less on July 1 this year than last.

Soybean Stocks Large

Stocks of soybeans in all positions totaled 22,252,000 bushels on July 1. Farm stocks in 5 principal soybean-producing States were estimated by the Department of Agriculture at 7,565,000 bushels and stocks in country elevators and warehouses in 6 important States at 1,932,000 bushels. An additional 1,131,000 bushels were reported in commercial storage at terminal markets, and 11,624,000 bushels were reported on hand at crushing mills.

The total of 22,252,000 bushels, somewhat more than one-fourth of the total supply estimated to be available for crushing in the crop year 1941-42, is unusually large for this time of the year. Quarterly crushings in the first three quarters of the crop year have averaged 19.4 million bushels. Carry-over on October 1 usually is less than 1 million bushels.

Large Government Purchases of
Lard and Margarine

More than 80 million pounds of lard (including rendered pork fat) and nearly 18 million pounds of margarine were purchased in July by the Agricultural Marketing Administration. Purchases this year to August 1 totaled 471 million pounds for lard and 34 million pounds for margarine. Other purchases of fats and oils in July included more than 7 million pounds of salad oils and about 7.5 million pounds of animal fats and oils other than lard, chiefly oleo oil and edible tallow. Total purchases for the month exceeded 113 million pounds, equivalent to a weekly rate of 22.6 million pounds, slightly lower than the rate in June but much above the average rate during the first 5 months of the year.

Correction

The monthly consumption of glycerin by any manufacturer (except for certain purposes) is limited by order of the War Production Board to 70 percent of the average monthly rate of consumption in 1940, not in 1941 as stated on page 12 of the June Fats and Oils Situation. Consumption of glycerin was materially smaller in 1940 than in 1941.

OUTLOOK

Domestic Fat Production Increasing

Indications continue to point to an output of fats and oils from domestic materials in 1942 about 1 billion pounds greater than in 1941. Production of animal fats and oils, including farm butter and lard and reclaimed greases, may total about 7.2 billion pounds this year compared with 6.6 billion pounds in 1941. Major gains will occur in lard, tallow, and greases. Production of vegetable oils also will be materially higher, totaling possibly 3.2 billion pounds in 1942 compared with 2.8 billion pounds in 1941. Soybean oil, linseed oil, and corn oil will account for most of the increase in vegetable oil output. Total production of fats from domestic materials may amount to 10.4 billion pounds in 1942 compared with 9.4 billion pounds in 1941.

Even more striking gains in production are in prospect for 1943, although results will depend partly on the crop situation next summer. A partial indication for 1943 is given by the outlook for fat production in the 1942-43 crop year, now getting under way. Present reports indicate that production from domestic materials may total 11.9 billion pounds in this period, more than 2 billion pounds in excess of the output in the 1941-42 crop year. Butter as well as lard, tallow, and greases will share in the increases in animal-fat production in the 1942-43 season. Among the vegetable oils, cottonseed and peanut as well as soybean and linseed are expected to show substantial gains.

With prospective cotton production now indicated to be slightly over 13 million bales, factory output of crude cottonseed oil in 1942-43 may total about 1,450 million pounds. This compares with a production of 1,250 million pounds in 1941-42. Production of peanuts in 1942, according to the August 1 crop report, may total 2,800 million pounds. Approximately 1,450 million pounds of farmers' stock peanuts will be required for the "edible trade" and for seed and local uses. Thus, about 1,350 million pounds of farmers' stock peanuts would be available for crushing. This quantity of peanuts, together with low-grade shelled peanuts resold by cleaning and shelling establishments to crushing mills, would yield about 420 million pounds of peanut oil. Production of peanut oil in the 1941-42 season, now virtually completed, amounted to about 55 million pounds. According to August 1 indications soybean production will reach 186 million bushels, 74 percent more than last year. About 155 million bushels should be available for crushing, with a yield of approximately 1,400 million pounds of oil, almost double the probable yield from the 1941 crop. The outlook for linseed oil production remains practically unchanged from that given in the July issue of this report, when it was indicated that nearly 750 million pounds of linseed oil might be produced from domestic materials in the 1942-43 marketing year.

Large Domestic Production Needed

Despite the prospective record domestic production of fats and oils, a surplus of supplies over needs does not seem likely. Imports of fats and from the Far East have been greatly reduced in recent months, and scarcity of shipping space may restrict imports from other areas. Exports under lend-lease, moreover, will be materially greater in 1942-43 than in 1941-42. And with rising consumer purchasing power and maximum retail prices in effect, domestic consumption of fats and oils is expected to increase in the next several months unless restricted by Government action. In addition, larger-than-normal stocks of fats and oils are desirable in wartime as a reserve against possible unforeseen changes in supplies or requirements.

PRODUCTION AND UTILIZATION OF PEANUTS AND PEANUT OIL

1942 Acreage Double the Previous Peak

According to August 1 indications, about 4.2 million acres of peanuts will be picked and threshed in 1942, or a little more than twice the acreage in 1940, the previous peak year. This large increase represents the response to the need for greater production of domestic oil-bearing crops and the guarantee by the Department of Agriculture of prices for peanuts for oil averaging about 4 cents per pound, compared with an average level of about 2.5 cents per pound in recent years. Production will not increase in the same proportion as acreage, however. Yields per acre were unusually high in 1940, and 1942 increases in acreage are proportionately greater in the lower-yielding Oklahoma-Texas and southeastern peanut areas than in the Virginia-Carolina area. Production of peanuts picked and threshed may reach 2.8 billion pounds in 1942, 60 percent more than in 1940 and double the 1937-41 average.

The 1942 increase in acreage is reported to have been achieved largely by using idle land, with some shifting from corn and summer legumes. Any great additional increase would be largely at the expense of acreage in other crops.

Production of Peanut Oil to be Quintupled

Until 1934, peanut oil was produced in this country almost entirely as a byproduct of cleaning and shelling operations. Discolored, shriveled, and broken kernels produced in the shelling process and occasional lots of inferior in-the-hull peanuts were crushed as a salvage measure. Production of peanut oil from 1919-20 through 1933-34 averaged 14.6 million pounds annually. From 1934-35 to the present time, however, with the exception of 1936-37, a portion of each crop has been diverted to crushing for oil as a means of obtaining a greater total revenue from sale of the crop as a whole. During this period the average annual production of peanut oil was 76 million pounds. With the great increase in production of peanuts in 1942, and with only moderate increases in the requirements for seed, feed, farm household use, and the edible peanut trade, production of peanut oil from the crop of 1942 may rise to 420 million pounds, more than 5 times the average of recent years.

Most Peanut Oil Used in Shortening and Margarine

Although the best grades of peanut oil make excellent salad and cooking oils, and are particularly suitable for deep-fat frying, peanut oil is chiefly

used in the United States as an ingredient in margarine and shortening.
(See table 6.) It is used for the same purposes and in much the same way
as cottonseed oil, but usually commands a higher price.

Prices of peanut oil have been little affected in the past by changes
in domestic production or supply of peanut oil, having been determined mainly
by changes in the combined supply of cottonseed oil and lard. Even at the
comparatively high level of recent years, domestic production of peanut oil
has amounted only to about 6 percent of domestic consumption of cottonseed oil
and to less than 3 percent of domestic consumption of cottonseed oil and lard.

Peanuts a Versatile Crop

Peanuts can be turned to more different uses than most crops. On many
farms, particularly in Georgia and Alabama, they are used as a forage crop.
When the peanuts are ready the hogs are turned into the fields. "Hogging off"
saves the trouble and expense of harvesting and is encouraged by weedy, or
"grassy," fields and by high prices for hogs in relation to peanut prices.
When peanuts are not hogged off but are dug and picked or threshed, the vines
make good hay after the nuts have been removed, and hogs may be turned into
the field to glean the peanuts missed in harvesting. The picked or threshed
peanuts may be fed to livestock and may be kept for food on the farms where
they were grown, but the great bulk of the crop is sold to mills. Relatively
few peanuts are crushed for oil and meal in normal years because they command
higher prices when prepared for the edible peanut trade. In recent years
about one-tenth of the peanuts taken by the edible peanut trade have been
cleaned; that is, prepared for roasting in the shell (see table 4). The rest
have been shelled. The major outlet for shelled peanuts is in peanut butter,
but large quantities are also used in candy bars and in roasting and salting
for retail distribution as salted peanuts. In addition, a considerable quantity
of shelled peanuts is used in bakery products. Disappearance of domestic
peanuts in the edible peanut trade more than doubled from 1920 to 1940.

Currently the demand for peanuts is greatly increased by wartime needs
for peanut oil and peanut meal. With reduced imports of vegetable oils and
increased export requirements under lend-lease, the need for all domestic fats
and oils is much greater than before. Peanut oil can be used not only in
edible products but also for industrial purposes. Sulphonated, it can be used
in place of sulphonated castor oil in textile manufacture. Although these
wartime needs are likely to be a temporary phase in the long-term development
of the demand for peanuts, they point to the desirability of a still greater
production of peanuts for oil in 1943. Large supplies of oil meals also are
needed to help maintain the large output of meat, dairy products, and animal
fats necessary for feeding our military forces and civilian population and
for helping to feed our Allies.

Large Acreage Suitable for Peanut Production

Peanuts are well-adapted to sandy and other light-textured soils in
the South. Perhaps one-fourth of the crop land in the 12 States where peanuts

are grown commercially, or roughly 35 million acres, is suitable for peanuts.
Peanuts have never occupied more than a small fraction of this potential
acreage, however, because of the competition of other crops, particularly
cotton, for the same land.

The acreage of peanuts picked and threshed averaged about 480,000 in
1909-13. Since then it has shown a constant upward trend, reaching 1,820,000
acres in 1937-41. Production increased in about the same proportion, rising
from 370 million pounds to 1,390 million pounds (farmers' stock peanuts).
Several factors appear to have been responsible for the increase. The spread
of the boll weevil through the Cotton Belt prior to 1920 decreased the yield
and profitability of cotton. Together with high prices for peanuts, the boll
weevil shared responsibility for a large-scale shift from cotton to peanuts in
southeastern Alabama and Southwestern Georgia about 1917. In recent years,
partly as a result of the peanut diversion programs beginning in 1934 and the
loss of export outlets for cotton, the ratio between prices received by farmer
for cotton and peanuts has become more favorable for peanuts. Demand for domestic peanuts was heightened by increases in import duties on peanuts in 1921
and 1922 and again in 1929 and 1930. After the latter increases, the rates
were at the prohibitive levels of 4.25 cents per pound for unshelled peanuts
and 7 cents for shelled. Imports since July 1, 1930 have averaged about 4
million pounds a year compared with 71 million pounds a year in the period
1922 to 1929.

                                          -- E. L. BURTIS

Table 2.- Peanuts, picked and threshed: Acreage, yield per acre,
production, and disposition, 1909-42

Crop of	Acreage	Yield per acre	Production	Total used for seed 1/	Used on farms where grown			Sold	Estimated commercial production 2/
					For seed	Fed and lost	Consumed in household		
	1,000 acres	Lb.	Mil. lb.	Mil. lb.	Mil. lb.	Mil. lb.	Mil. lb.	Mil. lb.	Mil. lb.
1909	537	660	355	38	30	10	16	298	---
1910	464	827	384	40	31	11	16	326	---
1911	472	775	366	41	32	10	16	307	---
1912	480	753	362	42	32	10	16	302	---
1913	465	824	383	46	36	10	16	321	---
1914	526	800	421	52	40	11	17	353	---
1915	617	779	481	66	51	12	19	399	---
1916	878	758	666	80	61	14	22	570	---
1917	1,314	752	989	82	62	16	23	887	---
1918	1,326	713	946	71	54	16	22	854	---
1919	957	719	688	74	57	16	19	596	562
1920	995	699	696	75	57	17	19	602	572
1921	980	692	678	66	51	16	21	590	562
1922	821	637	523	65	50	15	21	438	411
1923	797	713	568	82	63	15	21	470	439
1924	1,084	658	713	77	59	18	25	611	581
1925	996	725	722	71	55	15	22	630	599
1926	860	770	662	86	66	13	22	561	526
1927	1,086	777	844	92	70	15	26	733	693
1928	1,213	695	844	94	71	20	28	724	686
1929	1,262	712	898	86	65	19	28	787	748
1930	1,073	650	697	104	79	20	26	573	537
1931	1,440	733	1,056	117	89	20	34	913	864
1932	1,501	627	941	102	78	19	45	799	752
1933	1,217	673	820	116	88	19	41	671	628
1934	1,514	670	1,014	120	90	20	51	853	801
1935	1,497	770	1,153	129	92	22	47	992	924
1936	1,660	759	1,260	120	90	19	43	1,108	1,044
1937	1,538	802	1,233	132	92	20	40	1,081	999
1938	1,692	762	1,289	145	94	17	42	1,136	1,062
1939	1,906	636	1,212	146	90	20	45	1,057	961
1940 3/	2,040	858	1,750	141	100	21	45	1,585	1,540
1941 3/	1,914	772	1,477	214	104	18	43	4/ 1,312	4/ 1,180
1942 5/	4,173	671	2,800						

Data, 1909-40, except estimated commercial production, revised July 1942.
1/ The difference between total seed and seed used on farms where grown represents
peanuts purchased for seed and is duplicated under "Sold." 2/ Farmers' stock peanuts consumed by mills in the production of cleaned and shelled peanuts and crude
peanut oil. 3/ Preliminary. 4/ Estimate. 5/ Indicated August 1.

Table 3.- Peanuts, basis in the shell: Production, trade, stocks September 30, and apparent domestic disappearance, 1909-42

Crop year	Peanuts picked and threshed 1/	Imports 2/	Exports 2/	Reexports 2/	Net imports or net exports (-) 2/	Mill and warehouse stocks at end of period 3/	Apparent disappearance
	Mil. lb.	Mil. lb.	Mil. lb.	Mil. lb.	Mil. lb.	Mil. lb.	Mil. lb.
1909	355	35	4	1	30	----	385
1910	384	23	5	2	16	----	400
1911	366	17	6	1	10	----	376
1912	362	22	7	4/	15	----	376
1913	383	58	8	1	49	----	432
1914	421	29	6	2	21	----	442
1915	481	38	9	2	27	----	508
1916	666	49	22	4/	26	----	692
1917	989	113	12	1	100	----	1,089
1918	946	31	14	4/	17	----	963
1919	688	193	14	1	177	----	866
1920	696	69	13	1	55	----	751
1921	678	15	13	4/	1	----	680
1922	523	68	9	1	58	----	581
1923	568	76	4	2	70	----	638
1924	713	140	3	4	133	----	846
1925	722	54	4	5	45	----	767
1926	662	75	5	7	62	----	724
1927	844	96	5	5	86	----	931
1928	844	46	6	3	37	----	880
1929	898	5/ 15	4	2	5/ 10	----	908
1930	697	5/ 14	3	3	5/ 9	----	706
1931	1,056	5/ 2	3	2	5/ - 3	----	1,053
1932	941	5/ 4/	5	4/	5/ - 5	----	936
1933	820	5/ 1	1	----	5/ - 1	----	819
1934	1,014	4/	4/	----	4/	----	1,014
1935	1,153	4/	4/	----	4/	----	1,153
1936	1,260	2	4/	----	2	----	1,262
1937	1,233	6/ 3	1	----	6/ 3	145	1,235
1938	1,289	8	1	----	8	69	1,373
1939	1,212	9	1	----	8	222	1,067
1940	1,750	6	1	----	6	77	1,900
1941	7/1,477						
1942	8/2,800						

Continued -

Table 3.- Peanuts, basis in the shell: Production, trade, stocks September 30,
and apparent domestic disappearance, 1909-42 - Continued

Compiled as follows:
  Production and stocks, Bureau of Agricultural Economics. Production,
    1909-40, revised July 1942.
  Trade figures, Monthly Summary of Foreign Commerce of the United States
    and official records of the Bureau of the Census.
  Apparent disappearance computed from unrounded figures on production,
    trade, and stocks.
1/ Beginning of the picking and threshing season varies from August 1 in
southern Texas to November 1 in Virginia and North Carolina.
2/ Year beginning July 1. Imports for consumption beginning 1933.
3/ September 30. Farmers' stock peanuts. Comparable data for years prior to
1937 not available.
4/ Less than 500,000 pounds.
5/ January 1930-December 1933, includes imports of peanuts from the Philippine
Islands, considered as shelled nuts.
6/ Excludes 3,371,850 pounds "free for export."
7/ Preliminary.
8/ Indicated August 1.

Table 4.- Peanuts, farmers' stock basis: Crushings, disappearance in the edible trade, and stocks of milled peanuts on September 30, 1919-41

Year begin-ning October	Crushings			Disappearance of pea-nuts prepared for the edible trade			Mill and warehouse stocks at end of period			
	Farmers stock (in the shell)	Oil stock (shelled peanuts) 1/	Total	Cleaned (in the shell) 2/	Shelled 1/	Total	Oil stock peanuts 1/	Cleaned peanuts 2/	Shelled peanuts 1/	Total basis farmers' stock
	Mil. lb.	Mil. lb.	Mil. lb.	Mil. lb.	Mil. lb.	Mil. lb.	Mil. lb.	Mil. lb.	Mil. lb.	Mil. lb.
1919	10	25	35	---	---	---	---	---	---	---
1920	75	37	112	100	300	400	---	---	---	---
1921	84	31	115	80	320	400	---	---	---	---
1922	13	18	32	84	285	369	---	---	---	---
1923	2	17	18	101	335	436	---	---	---	---
1924	10	58	68	83	375	458	---	---	---	---
1925	8	42	50	97	445	542	---	---	---	---
1926	1	34	35	97	380	477	---	---	---	---
1927	20	41	61	90	560	650	---	---	---	---
1928	7	49	56	93	514	607	---	---	---	---
1929	29	92	121	85	560	645	---	---	---	---
1930	12	58	70	58	450	508	---	---	---	---
1931	9	43	51	82	690	772	---	---	---	---
1932	8	57	65	65	640	705	---	---	---	---
1933	3	42	45	67	550	617	---	---	---	---
1934	140	80	220	60	500	560	---	---	---	---
1935	182	58	240	66	633	699	---	---	---	---
1936	211	84	295	73	739	812	---	---	---	---
1937	195	57	252	74	707	781	4	13	88	105
1938	261	44	305	73	711	784	4	8	45	58
1939	74	52	126	71	729	800	3	8	94	106
1940	558	50	608	75	831	906	2	11	112	125
1941 3/	165	48	213	72	896	968				

Continued-

Table 4.- Peanuts, farmers' stock basis: Crushings, disappearance in
the edible trade, and stocks of milled peanuts
on September 30, 1919-41 -Continued

Compiled as follows:
    Crushings -
        1919-37, Bureau of the Census; 1938-41, Bureau of Agricultural Economics
        Peanut Stocks and Processing Report.
    Disappearance of peanuts prepared for the edible trade -
        1920-37, partly estimated. Based on shipments of cleaned and shelled
        peanuts from processing plants as reported by the Agricultural
        Marketing Administration for the crop year beginning August in
        the Southwestern area, September in the Southeastern area, and
        November in the Virginia-Carolina area.
        1938-41, Bureau of Agricultural Economics, Peanut Stocks and
        Processing Report.
    Stocks -
        Bureau of Agricultural Economics, Peanut Stocks and Processing
        Report. Stocks of oilstock peanuts are reported by producing
        plants only.

1/ Shelled peanuts converted to farmers' stock basis by multiplying
by 1.5.
2/ Cleaned peanuts converted to farmers' stock basis by multiplying by 1.05.
3/ Partly estimated.

Table 5.- Peanut oil, crude basis: Production, trade, stocks December 31, and apparent domestic disappearance, 1912-41

Year	Production 1/	Imports 2/	Exports	Reexports	Net imports	Stocks, Dec. 31	Apparent domestic disappearance
	Mil. lb.	Mil. lb.	Mil. lb.	Mil. lb.	Mil. lb.	Mil. lb.	Mil. lb.
1912	.5	7.6	-----	3/	7.6	-----	8.1
1913	-----	11.3	-----	3/	11.3	-----	-----
1914	1.0	7.4	-----	.1	7.3	-----	8.3
1915	-----	6.3	-----	.1	6.1	-----	-----
1916	28.5	15.7	-----	.2	15.5	-----	44.0
1917	50.5	27.4	-----	.1	27.3	-----	77.8
1918	95.9	68.5	-----	.1	68.4	-----	164.3
1919	87.6	154.1	4/ 4.3	.1	149.6	21.8	237.2
1920	13.1	95.1	1.4	3/	93.7	31.2	97.3
1921	33.2	3.0	1.7	.4	.9	18.9	46.4
1922	22.6	2.5	1.0	3/	1.5	2.7	40.4
1923	5.4	8.0	.2	.1	7.7	2.0	13.7
1924	6.7	15.4	3/	10.2	5.2	4.0	9.9
1925	15.2	3.0	-----	1.7	1.3	2.6	17.9
1926	10.6	8.3	-----	.3	8.0	2.3	18.9
1927	10.6	2.8	-----	.9	1.9	3.1	11.8
1928	12.4	4.7	-----	3/	4.7	3.1	17.1
1929	16.1	3.2	-----	.1	3.1	4.7	17.7
1930	25.5	15.6	-----	7.7	7.9	12.8	25.2
1931	13.7	14.9	-----	13.4	1.5	6.7	21.4
1932	12.8	1.5	-----	2.1	5/ - .6	3.6	15.3
1933	12.6	1.3	-----	3/	1.3	3.3	14.1
1934	47.0	2.7	-----	-----	2.7	27.2	25.9
1935	44.7	80.7	-----	-----	80.7	30.3	122.2
1936	70.2	49.0	-----	-----	49.0	29.2	120.3
1937	50.8	6/ 53.3	-----	-----	6/ 53.3	24.7	108.5
1938	78.2	15.6	-----	-----	15.6	27.6	90.8
1939	73.1	3.8	.3	-----	3.5	21.3	82.9
1940	83.9	3.1	2.9	-----	.3	43.6	61.8
1941	149.8	7/	7/	-----	7/	43.6	145.9

- Continued

Table 5.-- Peanut oil, crude basis: Production, trade, stocks December 31,
and apparent domestic disappearance, 1912-41 - Continued

Compiled as follows:
     Production --
          1912-18, United States Tariff Commission, Certain Vegetable Oils,
          Report No. 41, Second Series, 1932.
     Production and stocks --
          1919-41, Bureau of the Census, Animal and Vegetable Fats and Oils.
          Stocks are crude and virgin plus refined converted to crude basis
          by dividing by 0.94.
     Trade figures -- Foreign Commerce and Navigation of the United States.
          Trade figures are crude and refined, not separately reported.
     Domestic disappearance computed from data on production, trade, and stocks.
     Totals computed from unrounded figures.
1/ From domestic material. It is believed that imported peanuts are not used
for crushing.
2/ 1912-33, general imports; beginning 1934, imports for consumption.
3/ Less than 50,000 pounds.
4/ July-December. Not separately reported prior to July 1919.
5/ Excess of reexports.
6/ Excludes free for export.
7/ Not available.

Table 6.- Peanut oil, crude basis: Factory consumption, by classes
of products, and apparent domestic disappearance, 1912-41

Year	Compounds and veg-etable cooking fats	Margarine	Other edible products	Soap	Other industrial products	Loss including oil in foots	Total 1/	Apparent domestic disappearance
	Mil. lb.	Mil. lb.	Mil. lb.	Mil. lb.	Mil. lb.	Mil. lb.	Mil. lb.	Mil. lb.
1912	1.7	---	---	2/	---	---	---	8.1
1913	---	3/ 4.2	---	---	---	---	---	---
1914	2.1	3/ 2.8	---	0.1	---	---	---	8.3
1915	---	3/ 5.3	---	---	---	---	---	---
1916	17.9	3/ 10.5	---	1.2	---	---	---	44.0
1917	12.2	3/ 21.6	---	15.1	---	---	---	77.8
1918	27.9	3/ 38.8	---	---	---	---	---	164.3
1919	---	3/ 48.3	---	3.1	---	---	---	237.2
1920	48.2	3/ 16.3	---	---	---	---	---	97.3
1921	15.8	3/ 11.6	---	11.0	---	---	---	46.4
1922	9.8	8.2	---	6.7	---	---	---	40.4
1923	3.8	6.0	---	6.9	---	---	---	13.7
1924	---	5.1	---	5.0	---	---	---	9.9
1925	---	4.8	---	---	---	---	---	17.9
1926	---	5.2	---	3.0	---	---	---	18.9
1927	---	4.7	---	2.0	---	---	---	11.8
1928	---	6.3	---	3.0	---	---	---	17.1
1929	---	6.3	---	1.7	---	---	---	17.7
1930	---	5.8	---	1.5	---	---	---	25.2
1931	6.0	4.6	1.4	.2	.1	1.2	13.5	21.4
1932	3.5	2.5	1.2	.3	2/	1.1	8.6	15.3
1933	3.3	2.6	1.3	.5	2/	1.1	8.9	14.1
1934	8.8	2.7	.9	.1	.1	2.4	15.0	25.9
1935	90.9	4.4	3.6	.8	.2	9.6	109.4	122.2
1936	88.5	4.1	2.4	1.7	2/	6.9	103.7	120.3
1937	58.1	2.9	1.9	.8	2/	3.7	67.5	108.5
1938	52.4	3.6	1.9	.5	2/	4.0	62.5	90.8
1939	51.7	2.4	8.7	.8	.2	3.3	67.1	82.9
1940	22.5	1.7	9.7	.4	1.3	3.8	39.5	61.8
1941	81.9	2.2	18.1	.6	5.1	6.4	114.3	145.9

Continued -

Compiled as follows:
   Compounds and vegetable cooking fats and soap -
      1912-30, United States Tariff Commission, Certain Vegetable Oils,
      Report No. 41, Second Series 1932. Data for missing years not available.
      1931-41, Bureau of the Census, Animal and Vegetable Fats and Oils.
   Margarine -
      1913-16 and 1920-41, Bureau of Internal Revenue; 1917-19, Institute of
      Margarine Manufacturers.
   All other data on factory consumption, Bureau of the Census. Not reported
      prior to 1931.
   Apparent domestic disappearance computed from data on production, trade,
      and stocks (table 5).
1/ Computed from unrounded numbers.
2/ Less than 50,000 pounds.
3/ Year beginning July.

Table 7.- Prices of specified oil-bearing materials,
July 1940 and 1941, May-July 1942

Item	Unit	July		1942		
		1940	1941	May	June	July
		Dollars	Dollars	Dollars	Dollars	Dollars
Castor beans, Brazilian shipment, C.&f., New York	Long ton	48.00	70.38	99.31 1/	75.00 1/	75.00
Cottonseed, U.S. farm price	Short ton	22.60	35.90	43.99	43.87	43.20
Flaxseed, No. 1 Minneapolis	Bu.	1.58	1.92	2.58	2.54	2.46
Flaxseed, U.S. farm price	"	1.44	1.71	2.43	2.35	2.28
Peanuts (for nuts and oil), U.S. farm price	100 lb.	3.42	4.16	6.30	5.51	5.59
Peanuts for oil, delivered designated agencies	"	---	---	4.11	---	---
Soybeans, No. 2 Yellow, Chicago	Bu.	.82	1.50	1.80	1.72	1.74
Soybeans, U.S. farm price	"	.73	1.30	1.73	1.63	1.62

Compiled from Oil, Paint and Drug Reporter, Daily Trade Bulletin (Chicago), Chicago
Journal of Commerce, Daily Market Record (Minneapolis), and reports of the Bureau
of Agricultural Economics.
1/ F.o.b. Brazilian ports.

MONTELL OGDON
FOREIGN AGR'L RELATIONS
U S DEPT OF AGRICULTURE
FNG-MESS   WASHINGTON D C

Table 8.- Price per ton of specified oilseed meals,
July 1940 and 1941, May-July 1942

Item 1/	July		1942		
	1940	1941	May	June	July
	Dollars	Dollars	Dollars	Dollars	Dollars
Copra meal, Los Angeles	19.75	36.20	49.94	49.60	49.50
Cottonseed meal, 41 percent protein, Memphis	25.55	31.00	34.31	34.30	35.40
Cottonseed meal, 41 percent protein, Chicago	31.60	36.60	40.50	40.55	41.30
Linseed meal, 34 percent protein, Minneapolis	24.30	32.00	36.00	35.20	35.40
Linseed meal, 32 percent protein, New York	25.90	28.30	31.50	31.70	33.75
Peanut meal, 45 percent protein, f.o.b. southeastern mills	24.40	30.60	46.19	37.30	36.31
Soybean meal, 41 percent protein, Chicago	22.25	33.80	38.30	37.90	41.80

Compiled from records of the Agricultural Marketing Administration.
1/ Bagged carlots.

Lightning Source UK Ltd.
Milton Keynes UK
UKHW021851121118
332198UK00006B/355/P